13/09

BROWN V. THE BOARD OF EDUCATION

Essential Events

BROWN V. THE BOARD OF EDUCATION

BY MARTY GITLIN

Content Consultant
Cheryl Brown Henderson, President and CEO
Brown Foundation for Educational Equity, Excellence,
and Research

ABDO
Publishing Company

CREDITS

Published by ABDO Publishing Company, 8000 West 78th Street, Edina, Minnesota 55439. Copyright © 2008 by Abdo Consulting Group, Inc. International copyrights reserved in all countries. No part of this book may be reproduced in any form without written permission from the publisher. The Essential Library™ is a trademark and logo of ABDO Publishing Company.

Printed in the United States.

Editor: Rebecca Rowell
Cover Design: Becky Daum
Interior Design: Lindaanne Donohoe

Library of Congress Cataloging-in-Publication Data
Gitlin, Marty.
  Brown v. the Board of Education / Marty Gitlin.
    p. cm.—(Essential events)
  Includes bibliographical references and index.
  ISBN 978-1-59928-850-5
  1. Brown, Oliver, 1918—Trials, litigation, etc. 2. Topeka (Kan.). Board of Education—Trials, litigation, etc. 3. Segregation in education—Law and legislation—United States. [1. African Americans—Civil rights.]
  I. Title.

  KF228.B76G58 2008
  344.73'0798—dc22

                                                2007012003

TABLE OF CONTENTS

Chapter 1	Separate but Equal	6
Chapter 2	The Fight for School Desegregation Begins	16
Chapter 3	A Win in Delaware	26
Chapter 4	Challenging the Supreme Court	34
Chapter 5	The Supreme Court Rules on Brown	42
Chapter 6	All Deliberate Speed	50
Chapter 7	Little Rock	60
Chapter 8	The South Fights Desegregation	68
Chapter 9	Forced Integration	78
Chapter 10	Fifty Years of Brown	88
Timeline		96
Essential Facts		100
Additional Resources		102
Glossary		104
Source Notes		106
Index		110
About the Author		112

Black passengers sit in the back of a bus, while white passengers sit in front.

SEPARATE BUT EQUAL

Imagine not being able to obtain as good an education as other students in your city. Imagine not being able to attend a school with a gymnasium or multiple bathrooms because of the color of your skin. Consider what it would be like to walk an hour to school because the school only a few blocks from your house would not let you in due to your race. For decades, American schools were legally segregated, granting white students better and more educational opportunities than minorities. The court ruling that prevented millions of American minority children from receiving a quality education actually had nothing to do with schools. The U.S. Supreme Court created the "separate but equal" doctrine in the *Plessy v. Ferguson* case in 1896.

Homer Plessy was considered a Negro under Louisiana law, despite the fact that seven out of eight of his ancestors were white. As a Negro, the public places he could go were limited. He was supposed to sit in specific areas of public transportation, which were separate from those where whites could sit. In 1892, Plessy boarded a train and sat in a car reserved for white commuters. After being arrested, he appealed to the Louisiana Supreme Court, citing the Fourteenth Amendment. Passed in 1868, the Fourteenth Amendment extended the rights and privileges of citizenship

Homer Plessy's Arrest

Homer Plessy's stance against segregation was planned. His arrest was organized by anti-segregationists. Plessy was selected for the legal fight because he could pass for white with his light skin color, which proved an excellent test of the idea of segregation.

"All persons born or naturalized in the United States, and subject to the jurisdiction thereof, are citizens of the United States and of the State wherein they reside. No State shall make or enforce any law which shall abridge the privileges or immunities of citizens of the United States; nor shall any State deprive any person of life, liberty, or property, without due process of law; nor deny to any person within its jurisdiction the equal protection of the laws."[2]

—*Amendment Fourteen, Section One*

to all Americans, regardless of race or nationality.

The case landed in the U.S. Supreme Court, which upheld his conviction by a 7–1 vote. Associate Justice Henry Billings Brown stated that the purpose of the Fourteenth Amendment was to "enforce the absolute equality of the two races before the law," but that it "could not have been intended to abolish distinctions based on color." Justice Brown added, "If one race be inferior to the other socially, the Constitution of the United States cannot put them upon the same plane."[1] In other words, Justice Brown was supporting the continued separation of people in public places on the basis of race.

The concept of "separate but equal" was born. The doctrine was used particularly in the South as a tool to limit the social and political influence of blacks. The Supreme Court's ruling gave power to individual states to ban blacks and other minorities from public places, including restaurants, terminals, and beaches.

They were forced to drink from separate water fountains, use separate rest rooms, and sit in the back of buses.

Most damaging was that "separate but equal" created racially segregated schools. The ruling had a major flaw beyond its general unfairness: schools attended by blacks were vastly inferior to those attended by whites. Not only were students separated, the schools they attended and educations they received generally were not equal. Prior to the *Plessy* ruling, the education level of black children in the South was already lower than that of their northern counterparts at the end of the Civil War. This was because black children in the South had been enslaved and were not taught to read or write.

The U.S. Congress created the Freedman's Bureau on March 3, 1865, to provide support to those freed from slavery, including rations, clothing, medicine, and education. By 1870, only 25 percent of school-age African Americans were attending schools. The organization was disbanded two years later. Rather than place African-American children in schools attended by whites, southern states—those that had been part of the Confederacy—opened and financed separate schools for them. This was the practice for several generations. However, school segregation was not practiced only in the South. Seventeen states still operated segregated school systems when World War II ended in 1945.

While the number of students attending schools rose dramatically throughout the twentieth century, and the quality of education improved, schools for African-American children never approached equality. In 1890, only 4 percent of high school-age African-American children attended school. By 1930, this number increased to 50 percent. State and local boards of education took steps to monitor and improve both instructors and curriculum.

Teaching in the South

Teachers who educated African Americans before the Civil War shared a particular trait: courage. Early in the nineteenth century, no public school in the South admitted black children and anyone caught teaching them to read or write was punished, run out of town, or killed.

Margaret Douglass of Norfolk, Virginia, learned this firsthand. When she was discovered teaching black children in the early 1800s, Douglass was convicted and sent to jail. Other brave teachers ran secret schools at night to avoid being caught.

Southern slaveholders did not want their captives educated because they believed they would be more likely to seek freedom. Even the education of free blacks in the North was violently discouraged. In a letter to Harriet Beecher Stowe in 1853, abolitionist leader Frederick Douglass wrote,

I assert that poverty, ignorance, and degradation are the combined evils, or in other words, these constitute the social disease of free colored people of the United States. To deliver them from this triple malady, is to improve and deliver them, by which I mean simply to put them on an equal footing with their white fellow countrymen in the sacred right to 'Life, Liberty, and the pursuit of happiness.'[3]

As state and local governments poured money into their school systems, only a tiny percentage was intended for black schools.

Differences between schools for blacks and those for whites extended beyond the quality of education they were afforded. Even by the mid–1930s, when heating, indoor plumbing, and electricity were standard in the vast majority of public schools, such basics were lacking in many black schools. Their buildings were usually dilapidated.

Overcrowded classrooms and less–qualified, underpaid instructors also worsened the quality of education for many black students. So did having fewer subjects and extracurricular activities. Even daily transportation to schools, particularly in the South, was unavailable to them. As World War II ended, states with segregated schools spent $42 million on transporting white students to school and only $1 million doing the same for black students. Fortunately, the schools for African-American students had dedicated teachers. However, the teachers were treated differently. In 1945, teachers in black schools were

Differences in Education Spending

In 1910, the 11 southern states with segregated schools spent an average of $9.45 to educate each white child and $2.90 per African-American child. Thirty-five years later, states with segregated schools spent 50 percent less on black students than on white students.

paid 30 percent less than their counterparts at other public schools.

The unfairness of "separate but equal" in public schools prompted tests to its legality. One early case took place in Richmond County, Georgia, where the overcrowding of the black grammar school caused officials to close the black high school and use the space for younger children. Local churches were ordered to establish schools for the high school students. A group of black parents filed a lawsuit stating that in light of *Plessy v. Ferguson*, the white high school should be closed as well so that all children could receive equal educational opportunities.

When it came to race relations and education, the court system was not ready for fairness. In a unanimous decision, the U.S. Supreme Court ruled that public education was a matter controlled by the states.

Opponents of segregation fared no better in 1908 after Kentucky passed a law mandating that schools could enroll students of both races only if they attended classes at least 25 miles (40 km) apart. In effect, this prevented integrated schools. The state was sued by Berea College, a private and integrated school. Though judged excessive, the 25-mile (40-km) law was upheld, opening the door for states to force segregation upon schools that wished to be integrated.

States did prevent integration. In another challenge, though not involving a black student, the father of a Chinese-American girl named Martha Lum tried to enroll his daughter in a neighborhood white school in Mississippi in 1927. Mr. Lum was aware of the terrible conditions of the local black school. The local school board denied his request.

The Lums were not challenging the idea of separate but equal, but hoping Martha would not be segregated since she was not black. The family appealed to the U.S. Supreme Court, which again ruled that states had the right to regulate their own schools.

The tide began to turn in the early 1930s, thanks to African-American lawyers Charles Hamilton Houston and Thurgood Marshall. Houston was the dean of Howard University Law School, founded specifically for blacks after the Civil War. Marshall graduated from Howard University in 1933. He had attended a segregated high school in Baltimore, Maryland, and then Howard University after being denied enrollment at the University of Maryland.

When Donald Murray was turned down by the University of Maryland School of Law because of his race, Houston and Marshall sprang into action. They argued that because Maryland had no law school for blacks, Murray was denied that opportunity even under the separate-but-equal doctrine. This was one of the first victories for school integration in higher education. The Baltimore court ruled that the law school had to admit Murray.

That same summer, Lloyd Lionel Gaines applied to the University of Missouri School of Law and was denied entrance. Houston again took up the cause, but the Missouri court ruled against Gaines. He appealed to the U.S. Supreme Court. The Court reversed the state's decision, ruling that because Missouri did not have a law school for blacks, the law school had to admit Gaines.

Murray's Legacy

Donald Murray's grand-daughter, Alana, graduated from the University of Maryland and is a noted speaker on the subjects of education and civil rights.

A third challenge was brought against the University of Texas in Austin when Heman Sweat was denied admission to the university's law school. The U.S. Supreme Court unanimously ruled in favor of Sweat.

These rulings loosened segregation's stronghold just a bit. However, inequality in the states' school systems was not weakened at all. Further challenges would be needed to make that happen. ⌐

Thurgood Marshall fought for desegregation for years.
He was instrumental in the integration of public schools in the United States.

The case Brown v. Board of Education *is named for Oliver L. Brown, one of several plaintiffs fighting segregation on behalf of their elementary-age children.*

THE FIGHT FOR SCHOOL DESEGREGATION BEGINS

While the *Murray, Gaines,* and *Sweat* cases helped in the fight against desegregation, the rulings in these cases applied only to three universities. More challenges were needed to fight the practice of segregation and provide equal facilities and educational opportunities to all American school children, regardless of color.

The National Association for the Advancement of Colored People (NAACP) was crucial in the fight against segregation. Charles Hamilton Houston and Thurgood Marshall were part of the NAACP's legal team. Their skills and hard work already had led to victories that integrated colleges. Their continued work, along with the efforts of NAACP members and countless individuals and families, would eventually lead to desegregation nationwide. Five lawsuits would ultimately lead to the landmark decision of *Brown v. Board of Education*.

Filing a lawsuit was part of a plan conceived and put into action by members of the Topeka, Kansas, chapter of the NAACP. Junior high schools and high schools were integrated in Topeka. The goal of the plan was to integrate elementary schools. After two years of failing to persuade school officials to desegregate

Preserving *Brown's* History

In 1992, the Brown Foundation in Topeka, Kansas, worked with the United States Congress to establish a national park to tell the story of *Brown v. Board of Education*. The park is located on the site of what was formerly Monroe Elementary School, one of the four schools for African-American children in Topeka before the Supreme Court's decision in *Brown*. The *Brown v. Board of Education* National Historic Site Act was passed in October 1992.

NAACP Legal and Educational Defense Fund

Thurgood Marshall and the other NAACP lawyers who worked on the cases of *Brown v. Board of Education* were part of the NAACP's Legal and Educational Defense Fund (LDF). Founded in 1940 with Marshall's guidance, the LDF's main goal was to give poor African Americans legal assistance. The LDF continues today, focusing on four areas: education, voter protection, economic justice, and criminal justice. The LDF does its work with the following mission:

"The NAACP Legal Defense and Educational Fund is America's legal counsel on issues of race. Through advocacy and litigation, LDF focuses on issues of education, voter protection, economic justice and criminal justice. We encourage students to embark on careers in the public interest through scholarship and internship programs. LDF pursues racial justice to move our nation toward a society that fulfills the promise of equality for all Americans."[5]

Topeka's elementary schools, Chapter President McKinley Burnett made a final attempt via a lawsuit.

NAACP members and friends recruited 13 parents (representing 20 children) to be plaintiffs in the case. These parents tried to enroll their children in the nearest segregated school. Once denied, the parents notified the NAACP, which gave the attorneys documentation needed to file the lawsuit.

The case focused on the fact that, even though black schools in Topeka had equal facilities and teacher salaries, programs and textbooks were not equally available. In addition, there were 18 elementary schools for whites, but only four for blacks. For many black children, attending a neighborhood school was impossible.

The NAACP filed the case *Oliver L. Brown et al. v. the Board of Education of Topeka (KS) et al.* February 28, 1951. The *et al.* means "and others." Oliver Brown was designated the lead plaintiff because he was the only man named in the case.

The case was tried in the district court, which ruled in favor of the school board. The NAACP appealed to the U.S. Supreme Court. The case would eventually be heard by the Supreme Court, but not on its own. *Brown* would be combined with four other NAACP cases.

While Burnett and other Topeka NAACP members worked on the *Brown* case, Thurgood Marshall was busy with another desegregation-related legal battle in Clarendon County, South Carolina. In 1947, Levi Pearson filed a lawsuit against the county's school board for not offering equal transportation opportunities for his three children. The school board provided 30 buses to transport white students to school, but it refused to have buses for black students. Pearson's children were forced to walk nine miles (14.5 km) to school. Other black children had the same issue. Not having an easy way to get to school caused rampant truancy and a dropout rate that left one-third of all black students in the district unable to read or write. The lawsuit was thrown out on a technicality.

When the Pearson case fell apart, a second case was filed in Clarendon County. Reverend J.A. DeLaine was the principal of Scotts Branch School, an all-black school in Clarendon County. The county school system provided buses for white students. DeLaine asked the school system to bus black students. The school system refused. The NAACP and Marshall got involved in 1949. They ultimately represented a case that went beyond transportation to ask for equal educational opportunities. The school board spent $179 a year to educate each white child and only $43 a year for each black child. In addition,

Kenneth Clark's Research and Testimony

Psychologist Kenneth Clark could not physically show the effect segregation had had on the children he studied, so instead he put dolls on the witness stand. During the Clarendon County case, Clark testified that he had used dolls in his research. Working one-on-one with black children, he had shown them both a black doll and white doll, asking the children which they liked best, which was nicer, and which was more fun to play with.

Most often, the children identified the white doll as being nicer and more enjoyable to be with. Clark concluded that the self-image of black children, even those as young as three years old, had been damaged. He reasoned that their preference for the white doll indicated their unhappiness with their own racial backgrounds.

Clark further pointed out that the children's negative feelings about their race was a result of living in a segregated society, one they felt judged them as inferior. Clark interviewed 16 African-American children in Clarendon County. In that group, 11 cited the black doll as bad and 10 of them judged the white doll as good. Clark's findings helped pave the way for courts to admit the psychological harm of segregated schools on black children.

black students were forced to use outhouses and drink from metal buckets. And despite the fact that they were much poorer than white students, black students had to pay for textbooks and heat in the schools while the white students attended their schools for free.

The district court in South Carolina heard the case May 28, 1951. School board lawyer Robert Figg claimed the governor was ready to make sweeping changes that would dramatically improve black schools. Marshall pushed for integration, arguing that any segregated school, regardless of changes made, provided blacks with an inferior education. Marshall called Kenneth Clark, an educational psychologist, to the witness stand. Clark testified that segregation harmed children. He had examined black students in Clarendon County and explained that a typical student had "basic feelings of inferiority, conflict, confusion in his self-image, resentment, hostility towards himself [and] whites."[1]

In his closing argument, Marshall reinforced Clark's view, saying,

Briggs v. Elliott

Reverend J.A. DeLaine of South Carolina created a petition that 20 Clarendon County parents would eventually sign in support of the case against the county school system. *Briggs et al. v. Elliott et al.* is named for the first two signers: Harry and Eliza Briggs.

Kenneth Clark's studies with black children determined that segregation was detrimental to them. His testimony to the Brown case was important.

The Negro child is made to go to an inferior school; he is branded in his own mind as inferior. This sets up a roadblock in his mind which prevents his ever feeling he is equal ... there is no relief for the Negro children of Clarendon County except to be permitted to attend existing and superior white schools. [2]

The court ruled against Marshall, but he would use the same arguments with the U.S. Supreme Court two years later, tying it in with *Brown v. Board of Education*.

Because he was busy with the Clarendon County case, Marshall had two assistants, Robert Carter and Jack Greenberg, handle the *Brown* case in Topeka. The highlight of the testimony in Topeka was that of Louisa Holt, a psychology professor at the University of Kansas. She said,

> *The fact that it [school segregation] is enforced, that it is legal, has more importance than the mere fact of segregation by itself does because this gives legal and official sanction to a policy which is inevitably interpreted both by white and by Negroes as denoting the inferiority of the Negro group.*[3]

Despite this strong testimony, the Topeka federal district court was simply not ready for drastic change. The NAACP lost the *Brown* case. The court believed that the Topeka schools provided a relatively equal quality of education. However, the court's official opinion essentially admitted that segregation was bad for children,

Topeka Schools Today
Today, Topeka schools are among the most racially diverse in the country. At a time when U.S. schools are becoming increasingly segregated, a typical white Topeka student attends classes that are 50 percent nonwhite.

and this statement would later be used in the Supreme Court to change history. Written by Walter A. Huxman, presiding federal judge, the court opinion states,

> *Segregation of white and colored children in public schools has a detrimental effect upon the colored children. ... The impact is greater when it has the sanction of the law; for the policy of separating the races is usually interpreted as denoting the inferiority of the Negro group.*[4]

Though the case was defeated, the momentum created by Thurgood Marshall and the rest of the NAACP legal team could not be slowed. Before the end of the 1951–1952 school year, the U.S. Supreme Court had agreed to hear cases from South Carolina, Kansas, Delaware, Virginia, and Washington, D.C. The country would never be the same. ⟶

Lucinda Todd was the first parent of the 13 named in the Brown case to volunteer to test the separate-but-equal doctrine that kept her daughter, Nancy, and other black children from attending Topeka's white elementary schools.

The Robert Russa Moton High School auditorium used by the defense in the
Brown v. Board of Education *case*

A Win in Delaware

By the early 1950s, patience among
African-Americans regarding school
segregation began to run out. It was being challenged in
many areas of the country. Two more court cases were
eventually added as ammunition to *Brown v. Board of*

Education and the Clarendon County case when the U.S. Supreme Court heard arguments on the issue.

One lawsuit was in Delaware. Ethel Belton and other black citizens of Claymont sued the state because of the distance their children had to travel to school and the poor quality of the school. Sara Bulah and a group of African-American parents in nearby Hockessin also sued the state for transportation and better schools. Two buses actually passed Bulah's house. The drivers simply refused to pick up her child. The federal district court in Delaware opened the case in Wilmington on October 22, 1951. Thurgood Marshall and the NAACP legal team represented the plaintiffs. Witnesses spoke of the horrible conditions of the schools attended by black children. For example, one school had no gymnasium, no water fountain, and no nurse's office. In addition, there was only one toilet available in the entire building for students and teachers to share.

Expert witnesses testified about the psychological and emotional damage inflicted upon black students in segregated schools. Prominent

Jim Crow

The term "Jim Crow laws" has been used to describe the segregation laws, rules, and customs that dominated the South from the late 1800s to the mid-1960s. The term actually comes from the song "Jim Crow" about a highly exaggerated, stereotyped black character.

Dr. Frederic Wertham

An expert witness for the plaintiff in the Delaware case *Belton (Bulah) v. Gebhart,* Dr. Frederic Wertham was later famous for writing about what he perceived were the harmful effects of comic books on American children.

psychologist and author Frederic Wertham offered that even if genius physicist Albert Einstein taught at segregated black schools, the education would still remain inferior. "It is the fact of segregation in general and the problems that come out of it that to my mind is anti-educational," Wertham argued.

He added that segregation caused an "unsolvable emotional conflict" that weakened a child's ability to learn and become a productive adult.[1]

Though the arguments used in Delaware proved similar to those in the school segregation cases in Kansas and South Carolina that had been lost, the NAACP won the Delaware lawsuit. The NAACP had an important victory in the spring of 1952 when the judge presiding over the case asserted that the idea of "separate but equal" established in *Plessy v. Ferguson* should be outlawed. However, he ruled that the only way this idea would be abolished was through the U.S. Supreme Court. The district court ruled that ordering the improvement of black schools in Delaware was not the answer. Instead, the court ordered that the 11 plaintiffs named in the two lawsuits be immediately admitted to

This monument commemorates the 1951 student walk-out led by Barbara Rose Johns at Moton High School.

local white schools. Thurgood Marshall declared the decision "the first real victory in our campaign to destroy segregation of American pupils in elementary and high schools."[2]

A similar case was filed in Prince Edward County, Virginia, when a group of 117 students at Robert R. Moton High School charged the county with providing an inferior education for its 450 black students. The plaintiffs refused to ask for improvements in the school but rather for immediate enrollment into the all-white schools.

Barbara Rose Johns

One day in 1950, 16-year-old Barbara Rose Johns went on a field trip with her classmates to the county's all-white high school. Barbara Rose could not believe what she saw: a wonderful library, labs and shops, new equipment throughout the building, and beautiful landscaping.

It was clear to the visiting students that the Prince Edward County schools were not equal. That fall, Barbara Rose shared her feelings with other students. They felt hurt and angry about the obvious school differences. Designed to house 180 students, their school had 450 students. Rather than build a new school, the school board erected three tar paper shacks next to the school.

Barbara Rose gave an impassioned speech during an assembly on April 23, 1951. Then she announced a strike of all students. None would return to class until their school was improved.

After NAACP lawyers got involved, the press began to print stories and display photos of Barbara Rose, who had impressed the media with her energy and passion in taking on the white men on the school board and uniting the black students and parents. The student strike lasted two weeks. This small step by a student was the start of the district and federal court cases against the Prince Edward County Board of Education.

The case began February 25, 1952. It was presented by NAACP attorneys who called on nationally known psychologist M. Brewster Smith, who was head of Vassar College's Department of Psychology. Smith put forth the most impressive arguments. He asserted that segregation tends to confirm black stereotypes in the minds of black children, saying,

"They are going to grow up with con-
ceptions of themselves as being, in
some way, not worthy."[3]

The Prince Edward County
attorneys argued that improvements
in black schools had been and would
continue to be made. They blamed
the NAACP for agitating blacks into
filing such lawsuits. The Virginia
court sided with the defendants,
stating that segregation in Virginia
was a way of life that did not hurt
either blacks or whites.

The plaintiffs were upset, but there
was no turning back. The NAACP

Moton Museum

Moton High School is now
a museum. Barbara Rose
Johns led a student strike
in protest of Moton's lesser
quality compared to the
all-white high school in
Prince Edward County,
Virginia. The Robert Russo
Moton Museum docu-
ments the events in Prince
Edward County that took
place in the 1950s that
contributed to integrated
public schools. The mu-
seum serves to educate
visitors and to honor those
who helped in the fight
against inequality and segregation in public schools.

lawyers pledged to take the case to the U.S. Supreme
Court. A month after legal proceedings began in that
Virginia courtroom, arguments began in the *Brown v.
Board of Education* case in Kansas. The district court heard
testimony from several parents. Silas Fleming stated
that children should be allowed to grow up together and
learn together, regardless of race. Only one of the 20
children represented in the case took the stand.

Attorney Jack Greenberg also called Hugh Speer,
head of the University of Kansas Department of

Education, to the witness stand. Speer said,

> If the colored children are denied the experience of
> associating with white children, who represented 90
> percent of our national society in which these colored
> children must live, then the colored child's curriculum is
> being greatly curtailed. The Topeka curriculum or any school
> curriculum cannot be equal under segregation.[4]

**Segregation in
Topeka Schools**

The case *Brown v. Board
of Education* was based on
the segregation of Topeka's
elementary schools. The
city's middle schools had
been integrated since
1941. Topeka High School
had been integrated since
the end of the nineteenth
century.

The district court ruled against
the NAACP, but only because of its
view that the education offered by
Topeka's black schools met the test
of being separate but equal. What
helped those who were fighting
against segregation was the court's
opinion that black children were
indeed being damaged emotionally
by attending segregated schools.
The district court's opinion was
essentially a recommendation that
the idea of separate but equal should
be challenged in the U.S. Supreme
Court. ⌐

*NAACP lawyer Jack Greenberg argued for school
desegregation in Brown v. Board of Education.*

The NAACP Educational Fund lawyers: Louis L. Redding, Robert L. Carter,
Oliver W. Hill, Thurgood Marshall, and Spotswood W. Robinson III

CHALLENGING THE
SUPREME COURT

While Thurgood Marshall was busy
arguing the Clarendon County case in
South Carolina, he followed what was happening in the
other lawsuits that would eventually challenge school

segregation in the U.S. Supreme Court. The showdown over the practice of separate but equal became a national issue when he finally filed the *Brown v. Board of Education* case. Marshall was ready to fight.

Marshall and his colleagues from the NAACP Legal Defense Fund met in New York late in the summer of 1952 to prepare for the legal battle that would take place in December. They scrutinized documents, often for 16 hours a day, to prepare to present the strongest argument for school desegregation.

Marshall was no stranger to the U.S. Supreme Court. He had won 11 of the 13 federal cases he had previously argued there. On this issue, Marshall offered that the only reason for upholding the notion of school segregation was "to find that for some reason Negroes are inferior to all other human beings."[1]

Marshall used the skills and knowledge of the lawyers who had argued the cases in Virginia, Delaware, and Kansas that led to this historic legal battle. Assistants Robert Carter, Spotswood Robinson,

Charles Hamilton Houston

Charles Hamilton Houston started the campaign to end segregation in public schools. His work for the cause was just one facet of his lifelong efforts to fight racial discrimination. Houston taught at and led the work that gained Howard University Law School accreditation by both the American Bar Association and the Association of American Law Schools. It was at Howard Law School that Houston met Thurgood Marshall, becoming both his teacher and mentor.

Oliver Hill, Jack Greenberg, and others studied previous Supreme Court and lower-court decisions that might be used as ammunition to convince the Court that "separate but equal" was illegal.

The NAACP legal team prepared thoroughly, holding a mock trial at Howard University School of Law. Professors played the roles of the justices, listening as Marshall and his associates presented their case. This allowed the lawyers to get an idea of the counterarguments and obstacles they might encounter during the trial.

Thurgood Marshall

Thurgood Marshall was the most important figure in abolishing school segregation. Marshall was born July 2, 1908, in Baltimore, Maryland. Marshall's father raised him to appreciate the U.S. Constitution and rules of law. His mother pawned her engagement and wedding rings to pay Marshall's law school tuition.

Marshall was denied admission to the University of Maryland School of Law because he was black. He enrolled at Howard University, studied the Constitution, and then fought successfully to overturn the 1898 Supreme Court ruling in *Plessy v. Ferguson* that legalized the idea of separate but equal schools for black and white students.

In 1933, Marshall successfully sued the University of Maryland, making it possible for black students to attend. He later became chief counsel for the NAACP and helped the United Nations draft a constitution for Ghana (now known as Tanzania).

Marshall was appointed to the U. S. Court of Appeals by President Kennedy. In 1965, President Johnson appointed him solicitor general. In 1967, Marshall became the first African-American justice in the U. S. Supreme Court, where he served until 1991. Marshall represented and won more cases before the Court than any other American.

Thurgood Marshall passed away January 24, 1993, at the age of 84.

When the trial started December 9, 1952, the NAACP attorneys were ready. The trial began in an ornate building of the Supreme Court in Washington, D.C., that had an inscription proclaiming "Equal Justice Under Law" over the entrance. Marshall, his legal associates, and anti-segregationists around the world hoped that those words were more than decoration.

The Supreme Court Building

The Supreme Court building's inner corridors showcase panels and medallions depicting some of the greatest lawmakers in human history, including Solomon, Moses, Confucius, and King John.

Each member of the team handled parts of the case with which he was most familiar. Carter argued against the ruling in Topeka that supposedly justified "separate but equal" with a decision based on the view that both schools offered equal educational opportunities. Carter said of black students,

> *They have been denied equal protection of the laws where the state requires segregated schools. It denies them equal opportunities which the Fourteenth Amendment adequately secures.*[2]

Marshall took over after Carter. He criticized Virginia's district court for suggesting that segregation was a matter for individual states to decide. When one

Supreme Court justice asked about previous decisions on school segregation, Marshall referred to the U.S. Constitution in his answer, stating, "This court has repeatedly said that these distinctions on the basis of race ... are odious and invidious"—they are distasteful and against American values.[3]

Renowned constitutional law attorney John W. Davis argued against Marshall. He talked about how South Carolina worked to improve black schools and how states had the right to classify individuals by race. He concluded by saying that "there is no reason assigned here why this Court or any other should reverse the findings of 90 years."[4]

The following day, Robinson presented his appeal in the Prince Edward County case. School board lawyer Justin Moore attempted to discredit the testimony of psychologist Kenneth Clark, saying Clark spent little time in the South and did not understand the value system there. He added that the

The NAACP

Founded February 12, 1909, the National Association for the Advancement of Colored People (NAACP) is the United States' oldest civil rights organization. While the NAACP is best known for its work toward the betterment of African Americans' lives, the organization represents all racial and ethnic minorities in the United States. The NAACP strives "to ensure the political, educational, social, and economic equality of rights of all persons and to eliminate racial hatred and racial discrimination."[5]

students at Moton High were not dissatisfied with the education but rather were persuaded by the NAACP to sue.

Another lawyer stated that the lower court was mistaken in its judgment because the school board was in the process of improving the black schools in the county. NAACP representative Greenberg argued that those plans were uncertain and that the district court was justified in ruling that the all-white schools were legally bound to enroll black students.

Bolling v. Sharpe

Bolling v. Sharpe, a Washington, D.C., case, was also argued during the *Brown v. Board of Education* hearings, though it was not part of *Brown*. Because the Fourteenth Amendment was not applicable in the District of Columbia, the Supreme Court decided this case separately from Brown. The Supreme Court ruling in this case, however, proved vital in integrating schools in the nation's capital.

The NAACP legal team also argued that segregation was especially harmful to younger students, stating,

> *It is at the elementary school or primary education level that children, along with their acquisition of facts and figures, integrate and formulate basic ideas and attitudes about the society in which they live.*
>
> *When these early attitudes are born and fashioned within a segregated educational framework, students of both the*

majority and minority groups are not only limited in a full and complete interchange of ideas and responses, but are confronted and influenced by value judgments, sanctioned by their society which establishes qualitative distinctions on the basis of race.

Education cannot be separated from the social environment in which the child lives. He cannot attend separate schools and learn the meaning of equality. Segregated education, particularly at the elementary level, where the emotional aspects of learning are tied up with the learning process itself, must and does have a definite and [negative] effect upon the Negro child.[6]

Marshall and his associates left the courtroom on December 11, 1952. They had all worked hard on the important case and looked forward to enjoying the holiday season. The men would have to wait until after Christmas for the Supreme Court's ruling. Little did they know that they would still be waiting for a ruling the following Christmas.

John W. Davis, left, and Thurgood Marshall were lawyers on opposite sides of the
battle for integration in public schools.

Members of the U.S. Supreme Court, 1953

THE SUPREME COURT
RULES ON *BROWN*

Whether it is legal to keep black and white students from learning together in school seems a simple case of fairness and equality. After all, the opening of the Declaration of Independence proclaims that "all men are created equal." But legal cases can be complicated. A court of law determines outcomes based on right and wrong, as well as on precedents, or previous rulings, set by courts. The Supreme Court justices had a lot to consider and debate when they gathered again early in 1953 to decide *Brown v. Board of Education*.

The justices reviewed transcripts of the arguments and lower-court decisions before discussing the case among themselves. They asked themselves a few questions: Was the Fourteenth Amendment intended to outlaw school segregation? Would the outcome simply change the lives of the students represented in the cases, or would it change the lives of all children across the entire educational system of the United States? If the Supreme Court determined that school segregation was illegal, what were its options? Would it order all segregated schools closed until integration plans were in place or give schools time to desegregate?

At first, the justices were divided. Chief Justice Fred Vinson and associate justices Stanley Forman Reed and

Supreme Court Proceedings

No witnesses are called to testify in Supreme Court cases. Hearings generally last no more than a few days. Lawyers are allowed to speak for one hour each, including time to refute arguments from opposing lawyers. The Supreme Court justices also use that time to question the lawyers.

Tom Clark were leaning against the NAACP. Justices
Hugo Black, William O. Douglas, Harold Burton, and
Sherman Minton were with the NAACP. Justices Felix
Frankfurter and Robert Jackson were uncertain. They
needed more time to decide because they were unsure
whether the Fourteenth Amendment guaranteed
integrated schools. That is, when the
amendment talked about equality, the
men were not clear that the idea of
educating blacks and whites together
was included. On June 8, 1953, the
two men requested another six
months to research and ponder the
answer to that question. The request
was granted.

Robert Jackson

Robert Jackson, one of the
Supreme Court justices,
was a key prosecution
lawyer in the famed
Nuremberg Trials of the
mid-1940s, after which
several key German Nazis
were hanged for war
crimes and crimes against
humanity before and dur-
ing World War II.

At first, Marshall and the NAACP attempted to
follow the same path they had used originally—they had
to prove that the Fourteenth Amendment guaranteed
integrated schools. But their research turned up no
such evidence. The amendment includes no references
to public schools—public education simply was not a
major issue in the 1860s when the amendment was
written. The men decided to take a different approach.
They would ask about the intent of the creators of the
Fourteenth Amendment. Was it to stamp out racial

inequality everywhere? Had it not already been determined that segregated schools were indeed unequal and that black children were damaged by their existence?

The Fourteenth Amendment guaranteed equal opportunity, but state-sponsored school segregation did not. Marshall helped draft a lengthy legal brief, explaining,

> The very purpose of the Thirteenth, Fourteenth, and Fifteenth Amendments was to effectuate a complete break with governmental action based on the established uses, customs and traditions of the slave era, to revolutionize the legal relationship between Negroes and whites, to destroy the inferior status of the Negro and place him upon a plane of complete equality with the white man.[1]

Unfortunately, the case was delayed a second time when Chief Justice Vinson suffered a heart attack. He died September 8, 1953. Earl Warren, governor of California, took his place. The NAACP wondered if a newcomer to the Supreme Court would favor radical change.

It took time for Warren to familiarize himself with the case. Reargument began December 7, 1953. The courtroom was packed. Marshall offered that the

Supreme Court had interpreted the Fourteenth Amendment incorrectly when it established the idea of "separate but equal" in *Plessy v. Ferguson* and allowed individual states to decide whether segregation was good or bad. Opposing, John W. Davis argued that the Supreme Court had stated that the separate-but-equal doctrine was legal in seven separate rulings. Davis asked the justices whether black students would really be better off sharing a classroom with a few white children.

Davis's points were strengthened by his associate J. Lindsay Almond:

With the help and the sympathy and the love and respect of the white

---

Reaction to *Brown*

The *Brown* ruling was generally hailed as a positive step in living out the creed that all men are created equal, except in the South. Two sample excerpts of newspaper editorials printed the day after the Court's monumental ruling show opposing views:

The Supreme Court's resolution yesterday of the school segregation cases affords all Americans an occasion for pride and gratification. … It will bring to an end a painful disparity between American principals and American practices.
—The Washington Post and Times Herald

Human blood may stain Southern soil in many places because of this decision, but the dark red stains of that blood will be on the marble steps of the United States Supreme Court building. … White and Negro children in the same schools will lead to miscegenation. Miscegenation leads to mixed marriages and mixed marriages lead to mongrelization of the human race.[2]
—Jackson (Miss.) Daily News

people of the South, the colored man has
risen under that educational process to a
place of eminence and respect throughout
this nation. It has served him well.[3]

The next day, Marshall appealed
not only to the legal senses of the
justices but also to their hearts and
feelings of righteousness, saying,

Vinson's Death

The death of Chief Justice
Vinson may very well have
helped the cause for school
integration. He was con-
sidered among the most
likely of the nine justices to
vote against the NAACP.

I got the feeling on hearing the discussion yesterday
that when you put a white child in a school with a whole
lot of colored children, the child would fall apart or
something. Everybody knows that's not true. Those same
kids in Virginia and South Carolina—and I have seen them
do it—they play in the streets together, they play on their
farms together, they go down the road together, they
separate to go to school, they come out of school and play
ball together. They have to be separated at school.[4]

On December 9, the courtroom cleared again. The
justices were left to render a decision. Warren was won
over to the side of desegregation by late February 1954,
joining all but Reed. Warren hoped the Court could
speak in a unified voice. He persuaded Reed to change
his view. By May, the decision was unanimous.

A black student attends class at a newly integrated school.

ALL DELIBERATE SPEED

ntil the Supreme Court's ruling on May 17, 1954, three words—separate but equal—had allowed schools across the United States to remain segregated for more than 50 years. After the

Supreme Court outlawed the practice, three different words would be used by those who wanted to keep white and black students apart: all deliberate speed.

In 1955, the Supreme Court used the term "all deliberate speed" to give school boards and communities time to desegregate their schools. It was understood that such a massive change would present many problems. Little did anyone realize that in the South, where racism was a major issue, it would be more than a decade before the process of school integration was truly achieved.

It was not physically difficult to bring black and white students into the same schools. The main obstacles to integration were the feelings of racism and ideas about how the races should interact. Also, the states felt they should have the right to run their school systems without interference from the federal government or Supreme Court. Because of this, southern school districts made almost no attempt to integrate immediately following the decision. Such attitudes came from the highest offices. One hundred congressmen from southern states—19 senators and 81

All Deliberate Speed

When Earl Warren retired from the U.S. Supreme Court, he acknowledged that "all deliberate speed" was chosen as a guideline because "there were so many blocks preventing an immediate solution of the thing in reality that the best we could look for would be a progression of action."[1]

representatives—drafted the "Southern Manifesto" in March 1956 in response to the Supreme Court's decision. The document expressed that the politicians did not want anyone telling them how to run their states:

> We regard the decision of the Supreme Court in the school cases as a clear abuse of judicial power. It climaxes a trend in the Federal judiciary undertaking to legislate, in derogation of the authority of Congress, and to encroach upon the reserved rights of the states and the people.
>
> The original Constitution does not mention education. Neither does the Fourteenth Amendment nor any other amendment. The debates preceding the submission of the Fourteenth Amendment clearly show that there was no intent that it should affect the systems of education maintained by the States. ...
>
> This unwarranted exercise of power by the Court, contrary to the Constitution, is creating chaos and confusion in the States principally affected. It is destroying the amicable relations between the white and Negro races that have been created through 90 years of patient effort by the good people of both races. It has planted hatred and suspicion where there has been heretofore friendship and understanding.[2]

Senator Strom Thurmon was one of the writers of the "Southern Manifesto" in protest to the Brown ruling.

In the South, segregation was not practiced only in schools. Separation of the races was a way of life. Signs declaring "Whites Only" hung above the entrances to restaurants, restrooms, bus terminals, and other public places. Blacks were forced to sit in the back of buses. They were forbidden to vote.

Many southerners feared that *Brown* was the first step toward complete integration. Though some people welcomed the change, resistance was widespread. North Carolina Senator Sam Ervin summed up the feelings of discontent in 1956, writing,

> *Racial segregation is not the offspring of racial bigotry or racial prejudice. It results from the exercise of a fundamental American freedom ... the freedom to select one's associates. This freedom is bottomed on a basic law of nature—the law that like seeks like. It is one of the most precious of human rights, because man finds his greatest happiness when he is among people of similar cultural, historical, and social background.[3]*

Integrationists argued that legal segregation, including that of schools, actually caused the differences Ervin wrote about. It was hoped that desegregation would bring the races closer together, but most southerners were not willing to find out. Segregationist John Bell Williams, representative of Mississippi, even coined the date of the Supreme Court ruling as "Black Monday" on the floor of Congress.

Mississippi had long been considered the most segregated and racist state. On average, Mississippi schools spent only 30 percent of their money on African-American students—less than other southern states.

To fight the Supreme Court's decision, White Citizens' Councils throughout the South, many of them members of the notorious and violent Ku Klux Klan, organized efforts to resist desegregation. Mississippi judge Thomas Pickens Brady even wrote *Black Monday*, a book in which he recommended an end to the NAACP, creation of a forty-ninth state for Negroes (Alaska and Hawaii were not granted statehood until 1959), and abolition of public schools.

Senator Long

Not all politicians in the South reacted to the Supreme Court decision on *Brown* with anger. Russell Long, a senator from Louisiana, stated, "My oath of office requires me to accept it as law. Every citizen is likewise bound by this oath of allegiance to his country. I urge all Southern officials to avoid any sort of rash or hasty action."[4]

Among the first tests of white acceptance to integration occurred at the college level. In 1956, Autherine Lucy enrolled at the University of Alabama with the hope of earning a degree in library science. Her attendance, however, was made impossible—even dangerous—because of her race.

When she attempted to go to class, students and other people converged on the school to protest. They shouted racial slurs, threw eggs and rocks, and blocked Lucy from entering school buildings. The riot prompted the university to expel Lucy February 6, 1956.

A limited number of grade schools did integrate in the South after the Supreme Court ruling, mostly in states that bordered the North, such as North Carolina. Two Arkansas districts with a tiny number of black students and a couple others in South Carolina integrated immediately following the *Brown* decision. Others in Arkansas and Tennessee did the same in 1955. But the vast majority of officials and parents in the Deep South remained against desegregation. To avoid integration, some districts even closed their public schools and urged white parents to send their children to private schools. Others simply did nothing.

These feelings about segregation were not limited to

Hoxie, Arkansas

Not many people have heard of the tiny Arkansas town of Hoxie. The town's stand against desegregation is one of courage. The school board of Hoxie was the first in the South to voluntarily integrate its schools in 1955. This alarmed the White Citizens' Council, which was formed to pressure school boards into resisting desegregation. Council members organized local citizens to try to force the school board to reverse its decision.

The five members of the school board and the superintendent stood firm. The NAACP and area black families supported the school board, which sought a court order to stop the segregationists. The federal government stepped in and legally changed state segregation laws. This drew Orval Faubus, governor of Arkansas, into the dispute, but it was too late. Hoxie had secured a place in American history as the first southern city to cooperate with the Supreme Court order.

Autherine Lucy, center, with Roy Wilkins, left, and Thurgood Marshall, hoped to earn a degree in library science from the University of Alabama, but protestors kept her from entering the school. The riot prompted school officials to expel Lucy.

the South. In northern states, such practices were more subtle and difficult to overturn. Many areas created smaller school districts that would cut out large black populations. Some districts even spent money on building new schools in particular areas. This

First Schools to Comply

The first schools to comply with the Supreme Court order were in the northern parts of the South. Cities such as Hoxie, Topeka, Baltimore, Louisville, and Washington, D.C., desegregated their schools for the 1954–1955 year.

prevented white and black students from becoming classmates.

Once *Brown* was decided, desegregation supporters found it was difficult to keep the press interested in reporting on the issue. While every attempt was being made to avoid desegregation, particularly in the South, media attention turned elsewhere—that is, until nine black students tried to enter Central High School in Little Rock, Arkansas. This is when the morality of segregation came to everyone's attention as the ugly face of racism was contrasted with a group of innocent students. ⌒

guage in *Plessy* v. *Ferguson* contrary to this finding is rejected.

We conclude that in the field of public education the doctrine of "separate but equal" has no place. Separate educational facilities are inherently unequal. Therefore, we hold that the plaintiffs and others similarly situated for whom the actions have been brought are, by reason of the segregation complained of, deprived of the equal protection of the laws guaranteed by the Fourteenth Amendment. This disposition makes unnecessary any discussion whether such segregation also violates the Due Process Clause of the Fourteenth Amendment.[12]

Because these are class actions, because of the wide applicability of this decision, and because of the great variety of local conditions, the formulation of decrees in these cases presents problems of considerable complexity. On reargument, the consideration of appropriate relief was necessarily subordinated to the primary question— the constitutionality of segregation in public education. We have now announced that such segregation is a denial of the equal protection of the laws. In order that we may have the full assistance of the parties in formulating decrees, the cases will be restored to the docket, and the parties are requested to present further argument on Questions 4 and 5 previously propounded by the Court for the reargument this Term.[13]   The Attorney General

---

[12] See *Bolling* v. *Sharpe, infra,* concerning the Due Process Clause of the Fifth Amendment.

[13] "4. Assuming it is decided that segregation in public schools violates the Fourteenth Amendment

"(a) would a decree necessarily follow providing that, within the limits set by normal geographic school districting, Negro children should forthwith be admitted to schools of their choice, or

"(b) may this Court, in the exercise of its equity powers, permit an effective gradual adjustment to be brought about from existing segregated systems to a system not based on color distinctions?

"5. On the assumption on which questions 4 (a) and (b) are

A page from the Supreme Court's ruling in the
Brown v. Board of Education *case*

Thurgood Marshall sits on the front steps of the Supreme Court with some of the students who integrated Central High School in Little Rock, Arkansas.

LITTLE ROCK

lizabeth Eckford was one of nine African-American students spotlighted in the violent event that defined the desegregation era. The focus of the nation turned to Little Rock in 1957. Little Rock's school board did not plan on the national attention when it announced in 1954 that it would comply with the *Brown* ruling. There were no guidelines for integrating schools, so Superintendent Virgil T. Blossom developed a plan that summer for the 1956 school year.

Two new high schools would house both white and black students. The junior high and elementary schools would be integrated soon thereafter. When the Supreme Court added the "all deliberate speed" mandate in 1955, Blossom announced that only one high school would be integrated with a limited number of black students. Black families reacted bitterly, saying that Blossom was stalling for time. One board member angrily expressed his belief that the new plan was "developed to provide as little integration as possible for as long as possible legally."[1]

When the NAACP forced a court decision that all Little Rock schools be integrated immediately, Central High School was ordered to admit blacks. In the spring of 1957, teachers at black-only Dunbar High School

The Price of Desegregation

Because they were black, several of the Little Rock Nine were forced to give up their extracurricular activities when they attended Central High School. Carlotta Walls and Ernest Green had been in the National Honor Society in their former high school. Green was also an excellent saxophone player but was not allowed to join Central's band. Jefferson Thomas was not allowed to run for the track team, though he was exceptionally fast.

created a list of possible transfers from a group of top academic achievers. Of the dozens of students offered to transfer, only nine were selected because of parents' fear of racist backlash.

The Little Rock Nine

For the nine black students who integrated Central High School in Little Rock, Arkansas, what they achieved at Central was only one of many successes in their lives:

Ernest Green served as assistant secretary of Urban Affairs under President Carter. He works as managing partner and vice president of Lehman Brothers, a financial services firm in Washington, D.C.

Elizabeth Eckford joined the Army and became a journalist. She is a part-time social worker.

Jefferson Thomas worked as an accountant for the U.S. Department of Defense.

Terrence Roberts is head of Antioch University's Department of Psychology and is in private practice as a clinical psychologist.

Carlotta Walls Lanie graduated from Michigan State University. She works in real estate in Colorado.

Minnijean Brown Trickey was a writer and social worker in Canada. She currently lives and works in Little Rock.

Gloria Ray Karlmark graduated from Illinois Technical College and received her post-graduate degree in Sweden. She is a prolific computer science writer who currently lives in the Netherlands.

Thelma Mothershed-Wair graduated from college, after which she began a teaching career. She also volunteered in a program for abused women.

Melba Pattillo Beals is an author and one-time journalist for *People* magazine and NBC. She also teaches in and is head of the Communications Department at Dominican University of California.

Blossom met with the chosen students late that summer. He warned the students that they would not be able to participate in extracurricular activities. Blossom claimed this was because they were transfer students, but they knew it was because of race. If Blossom's intention was to scare the students away, it did not work. They were undeterred.

Segregationists were detemined as

well. The newly formed Capital Citizens' Council worked throughout the summer to pressure Arkansas Governor Faubus to resist the Supreme Court's order. The organization held a dinner for 300 segregationists. Among the speakers was Georgia Governor Marvin Griffin. He exclaimed to cheering attendees, "People of Arkansas, join my people of Georgia in determined resistance to the crime of integration." Griffin then predicted the end of American democracy "if the South surrenders her schools to the operation of the federal government."[2]

Congressional Medal of Honor

America's highest civilian honor, the Congressional Gold Medal, was bestowed upon each of the Little Rock Nine in 1999. The award was given for their actions to integrate Central High School.

As the first day of school neared, the Mothers League went to court with the intent of halting the desegregation of Central High. Governor Faubus appeared as a witness, claiming both white and black teenagers had been purchasing guns and knives at a disturbing rate. He predicted violence. A court order was issued that stopped the integration.

That night, racists throughout Little Rock celebrated. They threw a rock through the window of local NAACP leader Daisy Bates's house that included a threatening note. The Federal Bureau of Investigation

(FBI) got involved. The FBI requested verification of the governor's statement about the purchasing of weapons. Faubus answered that his sources were vague. A federal judge ruled that integration must take place as planned.

During his 1956 campaign for reelection, Faubus declared that forced integration would not happen while he was governor. Faubus did his best to keep his word. He called out local National Guard troops to prevent the nine black students from entering Central. Faubus claimed he was attempting to prevent violence. A district court ordered the integration to proceed.

Hundreds of protesters converged on the school to prevent the nine students from entering. The parents of the nine black students worked out a plan with Blossom. They would drop off their children several blocks from the school, where they would receive a police escort the rest of the way. But the Eckford family had no phone, so they did not learn about the plan in advance. Elizabeth Eckford would have to make the trip

Famous Photograph

A photograph of Central High School student Hazel Massery yelling at Elizabeth Eckford of the Little Rock Nine as Eckford tried to walk to school while surrounded by an angry white mob became the most famous image of the conflict.

The shot appeared in newspapers worldwide. Years later, Massery apologized to Eckford. The two worked toward racial harmony. They even appeared together on the *Oprah Winfrey Show*.

LITTLE ROCK CENTRAL HIGH

RAY   ROBERTS   PATTILLO   THOMAS   WALLS

MOTHERSHED   BROWN   ECKFORD   GREEN

Known as the Little Rock Nine, these students integrated Little Rock Central High School under the protection of federal troops in 1957.

alone. She was faced with a mob of white segregationists when she arrived at school. Someone hurled a brick at the windshield of one of the cars transporting another one of the nine students. The students finally reached police protection, but the National Guard turned the students away once they reached the school.

Faubus refused to remove the National Guard. The black students received their school assignments from

Daisy Bates, but they were forced to work at their homes. Little Rock's mayor, Woodrow Mann, criticized Faubus, claiming that the governor invented trouble when there was none. The next morning, Mann found a cross burning on his front lawn.

In late September, President Eisenhower forced Faubus to remove the National Guard troops and allow the Little Rock Nine to attend Central. When they arrived September 22, a mob of more than 1,000 protesters attempted to block the doors of the school. Fortunately for the students, the mob mistook four African-American reporters as parents of the students and rushed to the reporters. This allowed the Little Rock Nine to enter the school through a side door.

Central High School was officially integrated. Though a few white students walked out in protest, others were friendly. One white girl said the grown-ups were to blame for the trouble. Adults throughout the nation would soon cause a lot more trouble.

Central High Update

Central High has changed considerably since integration. From 1994 to 1997, it had one white male, one black male, one white female, and one black female serve as student council president.

In addition to being a public school, Central is a National Historic Site. The site has a visitor's center, a permanent exhibit, special programs, and tours. A new visitor's center marked the fiftieth anniversary of the desegregation of Central High School.

Seven of the nine black students known as the Little Rock Nine walk to Central High School in Little Rock, Arkansas, under protection of armed members of the 101ˢᵗ U.S. Airborne Division, who ensured they would enter the school.

Governor George Wallace blocks the entrance to the University of Alabama.

THE SOUTH FIGHTS DESEGREGATION

In 1963, Alabama Governor George Wallace spoke passionately to a rowdy group of his citizens. Wallace embodied the cause for racial separation in the South. He emphasized defiantly,

I draw the line in the dust and toss the gauntlet before the feet of tyranny and I say segregation now, segregation tomorrow, segregation forever.[1]

He mellowed over the years and even received help from blacks in winning later elections. But the stand that he and many others took prevented a smooth transition of school desegregation for more than a decade after the Supreme Court's *Brown* decision.

Even Little Rock's Central High School experienced problems. After the 1957–1958 school year, during which the nine black students were taunted and threatened unmercifully, school board members and Governor Faubus went back to court in an attempt to reverse integration.

A federal district court ruled that further school desegregation should be put off until 1961. But a month

George Wallace Runs for Governor

George Wallace gave the following speech during his first campaign for governor of Alabama in 1958:

"During the next four years, many problems will arise in the matter of segregation and civil rights, as a result of judicial decisions. Having served as judge of the third judicial circuit of Alabama, I feel, my friends, that this judicial experience will be invaluable to me as your governor. … And I want to tell the good people of this state, as a judge of the third judicial circuit, if I didn't have what it took to treat a man fair, regardless of his color, then I don't have what it takes to be the governor of your great state.

I advocate hatred of no man, because hate will only compound the problems facing the South."[2]

before the new school year, a higher court reversed that decision, ruling,

> *The time has not come when an order of a federal court must be whittled away, watered down, or shamefully withdrawn in the face of violent and unlawful acts of individual citizens.*[3]

Faubus and state leaders decided to close Arkansas's schools. On the first scheduled day of school, more than 4,000 students had no classes. Central Baptist College formed an academy for displaced white students. Classes in the basics were even held briefly on television. The segregated classes were funded by money donated by white citizens, but the new school proved unable to run financially.

The U.S. Supreme Court once again ordered desegregation to continue in 1959. A small riot occurred when black students attempted to enter Central High School. It was stopped by local police. That was the year integration finally remained a way of life at Central.

Meanwhile, other areas of the South struggled with integration. People who wanted to keep schools segregated tried a number of different legal ways to get around the law. For example, in 1956, Senator Harry

F. Boyd of Virginia declared "massive resistance," a
series of laws to prevent integration. One law kept state
money from being used for integrated schools.
Another established the Pupil Placement Board to
decide where individual students would attend school.
The board chose schools based on each student's race.
Yet another law gave money to white students to attend
private all-white schools.

Late in 1956, the NAACP filed lawsuits throughout Virginia to force desegregation. The federal courts again
ordered schools in Warren County,
Charlottesville, Norfolk, and Arlington
to integrate. In his attempt to prevent
school desegregation, Governor Lindsay Almond closed the state's schools in
1958. The following January, the Supreme Court of
Virginia ruled massive resistance unconstitutional.
Governor Almond was forced to withdraw his support
for it. The three members of the Pupil Placement
Board resigned. Virginia's schools reopened in
February 1960.

The National Guard

Established in December
1636 in Massachusetts,
the National Guard is
older than the United
States of America.

Desegregation could be legally ordered, but the
government could not make people get over their racist
ideas. When Warren County High School reopened,

it was all black. All the parents of the white children opted to send them to John S. Mosby Academy, one of many private segregated schools established as part of massive resistance.

Eventually, white students began returning to the integrated school systems, but it took time. In fact, the Prince Edward County schools in Virginia were closed from 1959 until 1964 while white students attended the new Prince Edward Academy. Black parents were left to fend for themselves when it came to educating their children.

The practice of closing the doors to black students was not limited to elementary schools. Colleges in the South also worked to limit desegregation. Most noteworthy is the case of James Meredith, who attempted to integrate the University of Mississippi in 1962. Meredith applied for admission into the school in early 1961. He was turned down. He took his case to the Supreme Court, which ruled just three weeks before the 1962 school year began

Wallace's Stance on Integration

George Wallace spoke the following words against integration at the University of Alabama-Tuscaloosa:

"The unwelcomed, unwanted, unwarranted, and force-induced intrusion upon the campus of the University of Alabama today of the might of the central government offers frightful example of the oppression of the rights, privileges and sovereignty of this state by officers of the federal government."[4]

After winning his Supreme Court case against the University of Mississippi,
James Meredith became the first black student to enroll in the school.

that Meredith had the right to enroll. When he showed
up to class, the situation turned violent.

When federal marshals and Civil Rights Division
lawyers finally escorted Meredith in, a mob began to

form despite the group of marshals, border patrolmen, and federal prison guards—totaling nearly 500 men—gathered to protect him. The mob grew to about 2,000 people. They attacked the men with bricks, guns, bottles, and explosives. The marshals were under orders to avoid bloodshed at all costs, so they did not use their guns. The men tried to stop the violence with tear gas but could not. Eventually, President Kennedy ordered a massive show of force. He sent National Guard troops to the scene to end the violence, but not before 2 people died, 28 marshals were shot, and 160 people were injured—all because one black man was admitted into the University of Mississippi.

Not to be outdone in his defiance of

James Meredith

The civil rights journey of James Meredith did not end when he became the first black student at the University of Mississippi. In 1966, two years after graduation, he began his self-proclaimed "March Against Fear" from Memphis, Tennessee, to Jackson, Mississippi, to protest racism. Meredith showed courage by taking the long trip alone.

Soon after he began the journey, Meredith was shot and injured by a sniper. The incident added publicity and support to the cause. When they heard the news, civil rights leaders such as Martin Luther King Jr., Stokely Carmichael, and Floyd McKissick decided to continue the walk from Memphis to Jackson themselves. Meredith joined the group after he was released from the hospital and completed the march.

Meredith's ties with the University of Mississippi continued when his son enrolled. Joseph graduated in 2002 as a distinguished graduate, receiving a doctoral degree in business administration.

desegregation, a year later Wallace barred the entrance of the University of Alabama to black students Vivian Jones and James Hood. The two young people waited in a car as Nicholas Katzenbach, the deputy attorney general of the United States, spoke to Wallace, saying, "From the outset, Governor, all of us have known that the final chapter of this history will be the admission of these students."[5] Wallace still refused to enroll Jones and Hood, so federal troops were dispatched to the university. This time, however, there was no major violence. Immediately after the troops reached the school grounds, Wallace relented, and the black students entered.

National Civil Rights Museum

The National Civil Rights Museum has exhibits highlighting many civil rights milestones in the United States, including the *Brown* case and integration of Central High School. Located in Memphis, Tennessee, the museum is housed in the Lorraine Motel. The location was chosen as the site for the museum because of its place in American history. Civil rights leader Martin Luther King Jr. was assassinated at the Lorraine Motel on April 4, 1968.

Time and the softening of racist views eventually wore down southern segregationists. Even so, school districts remained racially divided. The demographics of many inner cities changed as many white families across the country took advantage of the post-World War II boom to move to newly developed suburban areas. Funding for mostly black schools was woefully lacking. The obstacles faced by African Americans growing up in the poverty of inner cities and a lack of a tax base to support quality education continued to create many hurdles on the road to equal education.

By the late 1960s and early 1970s, lawmakers began considering a new method of forced integration. They examined whether it was possible to send black students into mostly white schools and white students into mostly black schools. This would be done by busing them out of their districts and into others. The policy of busing created yet another conflict in the battle for educational equality. ⌒

Students of all ages needed protection when integrating schools. Marshals escorted first grader Ruby Bridges to her elementary school in New Orleans, Louisiana, where she was the only black student.

Black elementary school students arrive at their new school in Detroit in January 1976 as the court-ordered busing began.

FORCED INTEGRATION

*S*chool desegregation through much of the South was a painfully slow process. Some districts integrated peacefully and with relative speed, but others tried to circumvent the U.S. Supreme Court's order. Many areas used the "academy" option for white students to prevent race mixing. Tuition for these schools was set purposely cheap to allow any parents who preferred to keep their children out of what were now predominantly black public schools to do so with ease. Such inexpensive private schools popped up throughout the South. One state official in Mississippi bragged, "Anybody can open a private school in Mississippi, and there's nothing we can do about it."[1] There was no need for new schools to be constructed because white children attended classes in abandoned school buildings, church basements, factories, and community centers.

Not only did such schools pay for any percentage of tuition costs individual households could not afford, but the curriculum at the whites-only private schools reinforced the racist belief system that initially fueled segregation. A young student from a private academy near Jackson, Mississippi, said,

> *We were taught that Earl Warren is a Communist, that the Supreme Court is under Communist control, and*

Georgia Teachers and Education Association

Most black teachers were in favor of desegregated schools, even if it meant they would lose their jobs. In 1956, Georgia Governor Marvin Griffin proposed a bill that would make public schools private to preserve segregation. On April 13, the Georgia Teachers and Education Association, which represented 9,000 black teachers, met in Augusta and endorsed integration, asking for abandonment of the governor's private-schools bill.

that integration is a plot made up by Communists and Jews.[2]

Eventually, the racial barriers being broken down in the South worked their way into schools. The protests and court rulings that led to integration of public places softened the perception against desegregated schools. By the late 1960s, attempts by school boards to keep white and black students apart decreased dramatically. But by that time, another confrontation was emerging: busing.

The idea of busing to force integration was actually the result of all the effort being made not to integrate. In 1968, a federal district court in Virginia ruled that New Kent County's school board had not acted quickly enough to end segregation in its classrooms. The county had used an open-enrollment system in which parents could send their children to their school of choice. A black majority opted to attend all-black schools because those who chose otherwise were harassed and ridiculed.

School Desegregation in the South

It took about 15 years after the *Brown v. Board of Education* decision to achieve school desegregation in the South. According to various statistical surveys, nearly 80 percent of all black students attended schools that were 90 to 100 percent racial minority in 1968. That figure dropped to less than 25 percent four years later. In 1972, southern schools were by far the most integrated in the country.

In *Green v. County School Board of Kent County, Virginia*, the Supreme Court unanimously upheld the federal district court's belief that true integration was not progressing quickly enough and that the school board should proceed faster to achieve it. The Supreme Court suggested that the racial makeup of a county be reflected in the area school. It was the first legal attempt to force integration rather than simply end segregation.

A year later, the Supreme Court again acted to promote integration. The school board of Holmes County, Mississippi, had requested more time to achieve desegregation, but the Supreme Court was in no mood for more delays—its mandate for all deliberate speed had come down 15 years earlier. The decision in *Alexander v. Holmes County Board of Education* read,

> Under explicit holdings of this Court, the obligation of every school district is to terminate dual school systems at once and to operate now and hereafter only unitary schools. [4]

Green v. County School Board of Kent County, Virginia

Justice Brennan delivered the Supreme Court's opinion on *Green v. County School Board of Kent County, Virginia*. In the ruling, Brennan said, "The burden is on a school board to provide a plan that promises realistically to work now, and a plan that at this late date fails to provide meaningful assurance of prompt and effective disestablishment of a dual system is intolerable. ... A district court's obligation is to assess the effectiveness of the plan in light of the facts at hand and any alternatives which may be feasible and more promising, and to retain jurisdiction until it is clear that state-imposed segregation has been completely removed." [3]

The Supreme Court made its strongest effort to force integrated schools in 1971. A federal district court in Charlotte, North Carolina, ruled in 1970 that its schools must reflect the population ratio of 71 percent whites and 29 percent blacks. It further mandated that school districts could no longer be designed to separate the races. Most important, James McMillan, a district court judge, ordered that 13,000 students be transported by bus to ensure that each school was racially mixed. He had taken a step too far in the minds of many throughout the country.

The Supreme Court disagreed. When *Swann v. Charlotte–Mecklenburg Board of Education* was appealed, it marked the first time the Supreme Court

Anna Louise Day Hicks

No public figure symbolized the anti-busing sentiment in the late 1960s and 1970s more than Anna Louise Day Hicks. Elected to the Boston School Committee in 1961, Hicks refused to acknowledge that segregation was a problem despite the fact that 13 city schools were at least 90 percent black. Hicks strongly opposed busing. She felt the Boston schools were being blamed for the city's economic and social issues. Hicks founded and was president of the organization Restore Our Alienated Rights (ROAR) after busing was mandated in 1975. She was elected the first woman president of the Boston City Council a year later, greatly because of her stand on busing.

Hicks claimed that because the schools in Chinatown were 100 percent Chinese and other neighborhoods reflected their racial makeups, there was no reason that predominantly black neighborhoods should not have mostly black schools.

Paul Parks, a former Boston School Committee chairman and vice president of the Boston NAACP said of Hicks, "She was a tragic figure. She became an object of hate—and she asked for it."[5]

Anna Louise Day Hicks died in 2003 at 87.

promoted busing as a way of integrating schools in all-black or all-white districts.

Taking their cue from the Court, many districts throughout the country began implementing busing plans as a means of integrating their schools. Many major cities were segregated racially. Most African Americans in the late 1960s and early 1970s lived in poorer urban areas as a result of racism and lack of opportunity. It was believed that poor education systems in these areas handicapped African Americans and played a role in preventing them from reaching their potential. School boards in white suburban areas argued that the influx of underachieving students would downgrade their schools. Some black parents and officials did not want their kids to be viewed as unwanted guests in previously all-white schools.

Nowhere was the controversy more heated than in Boston, Massachusetts. In 1973, the Supreme Judicial Court of Massachusetts ordered Boston's School Committee to formulate a busing plan to be in place by the following September. A total of 19,000 of the city's 83,000 public-school students would have to be bused. The school board began notifying families of students' new school assignments. The reaction was angry and immediate. The state legislature began hearings with the intention of reversing what was known as the Racial Imbalance Act. On April 3, 1974, a crowd of about 25,000 people gathered at Boston Common to voice their displeasure.

The district court ruled in June that the Boston School Committee had been operating a dual school system and ordered it terminated. The court found particular high schools overcrowded and others underenrolled. The district court cited the Boston School Committee for dividing districts based on race. The district court also pointed out that African-American students often were locked out of schools that practiced open enrollment or experienced segregated classrooms, auditoriums, and gymnasiums. Wendell Arthur Garrity Jr., a federal district judge, wrote,

> *In sum, open enrollment as administered by the defendants became a device for separating the races and contributed significantly to the establishment of a dual school system.*[6]

Boston braced for trouble. The organization Return Our Alienated Rights (ROAR) called for a school boycott. When the first bus carrying black teenagers arrived at South Boston High from Roxbury, a mob of angry whites, most of them truant students, began

ROAR President Anna Louise Day Hicks, right, at an anti-busing rally in Boston, Massachusetts, May 2, 1973

yelling racial slurs and throwing rocks and bottles. Attendance that first day was down. Only 10 of the 525 white students scheduled to attend Roxbury went to class. Only 196 students of the 1,539 enrolled showed up to South Boston High that day.

When the Ku Klux Klan got involved, violence flared on both sides. After a group of 35 white youths beat up a 33-year-old Haitian immigrant, African Americans rioted in the streets and injured 38 white residents. Federal marshals and state police were sent to restore peace.

President Gerald Ford admitted that forced busing was a poor solution to the problem of integration. By 1977, after the Department of Implementation was made fully responsible for the integration process, Boston's schools began making tremendous progress educationally, attendance rose, and violence decreased.

Forced Busing

In addition to Charlotte and Boston, other large cities tried forced busing in the 1970s and early 1980s to integrate schools, including Cleveland, Pasadena, Richmond, San Francisco, and Wilmington. The practice received mixed results throughout the country.

The experience in Boston and throughout the nation resulted in questions about the effectiveness of busing as a means to integrate schools. In fact, the phenomenon of white flight into suburban areas and the continuing plight of many blacks living in poverty in inner cities have resulted in mostly segregated schools. Busing as a means to achieve integration has greatly disappeared. The belief has grown that only equality in life will achieve equality in education. This raises another question: How can a group of Americans achieve equality in life without equality in education?

Black students in Boston, Massachusetts, receive a police escort as part of forced
busing to integrate Boston's public schools.

*The Little Rock Nine celebrate at an unveiling of a
monument in their honor in 2005.*

FIFTY YEARS OF *BROWN*

Though the U.S. Supreme Court banned
segregation more than 50 years ago, it has
remained an issue for generations. When the *Brown v.
Board of Education* decision was commemorated in 2004,
opinions on the subject ranged from celebrating its
effect on American education to lamenting its

perceived failure to desegregate schools. Studies have
shown reality to be somewhere in between. In 1954,
40 percent of all American students attended legally
segregated schools. Most attended schools in the South,
but now the South features the least-segregated schools
in the country. In addition, studies show that southern
schools boast a higher percentage of interracial balance
in extracurricular activities than northern schools.

While the racial mix is somewhat
even in southern schools, the same
cannot be said for other schools
across the country. On average
nationally, the school a white student
attends is most likely to have at least a
25 percent minority enrollment. On
the other hand, segregation has
actually become more prominent
over the last two decades. Suburban
areas that are predominently white
have translated into 25 percent less
integration overall since 1970. The
disparity is greatest in northern
states, particularly in the Midwest.
When given choices, both white
parents and black parents often have

A Return to Segregation

When a lower federal
court ruled in 2001 that
the Charlotte-Mecklenburg
school district in North
Carolina had erased all
evidence of school segre-
gation, the school board
promptly adopted a pupil
assignment plan based
on parental choice. The
result is that 23 percent of
black students in that district now attend schools
with 90 percent or more
racial minority enrollment.

elected to send their children to schools where they will be in the majority.

Money also continues to be an issue for schools that are predominantly African American. Just as was the case a century ago, the majority of inner-city schools are still badly underfunded, overcrowded, and in disrepair. They also employ teachers who are less qualified and less experienced than those in predominantly white suburban schools. Most people in the education community do not blame fellow teachers for wanting to work in better-funded schools that are often closer to where they live. American education critic Jonathan Kozol says of public schools today,

Education and Class

The *Brown* decision is partially responsible for the significant rise in the African-American middle and upper classes. However, the social and economic differences between whites and blacks and the number of whites moving out of cities to the suburbs mean schools are often made up of mostly one race. Many studies have shown the gap has actually widened during the past two decades. Mostly black schools remain in the poorer rural areas of the South and urban inner cities throughout the country. Suburban areas and small towns house mostly white schools. Gary Orfield and John T. Yun of Harvard University's Civil Rights Project note:

Increased testing requirements for high school graduation, for passing from one grade to the next, and college entrance can only be fair if we offer equal preparation to children, regardless of skin color and language. Increasing segregation, however, pushes us in the opposite direction because it creates more unequal schools, particularly for low income minority children, who are the groups which most frequently receive low test scores.[1]

What seems unmistakable, but, oddly enough, is rarely said in public settings nowadays is that the nation, for all practice and intent, has turned its back upon the moral implications, if not the ramifications, of the Brown *decision.* [2]

Kozol has written about how schools in mostly white areas spend nearly twice as much on students as schools in minority areas. Similar disparities have been reported throughout the country. It is important to note that funding is based on tax revenues available to the school districts. Poverty results in less revenue, which means there is less money for schools in impoverished areas.

National Poverty Rates

Blacks experience the highest rate of poverty in America. In August 2006, the United States Census Bureau released the following poverty statistics:

Blacks: 24.9%
Hispanics: 21.8%
Asians: 11.1%
Non-Hispanic whites: 8.3%

Even with the continued differences between schools attended by black students and those attended by white students, a huge majority of black students in the United States are far better educated than their parents and grandparents were during the time of legal segregation. Many more black students go on to college, which means they can get better-paying and more prestigious jobs when they graduate. Civil rights legislation has resulted in more African-American doctors, lawyers, and politicians than ever before. Many feel this is the result of the increased black middle and upper classes. Regardless of race, however, those who remain in the inner cities with poorer schools are still likely to remain in poverty throughout their lives.

Since busing has been greatly dismissed as an effective tool to desegregate schools, many alternatives have been proposed to decrease the racial gap in American schools. Until the racial gap is closed, it is quite likely that students who live in poorer areas will continue to remain behind educationally. It has been proven that African Americans and Latinos in middle-class mostly white schools achieve far better results than those in underfunded predominantly minority schools.

The disparity between schools is a problem. In the 1950s and 1960s, there was a keen awareness of educational inequities from school segregation due to the publicity it

A Tale of Two Schools

In his writing about the disparity in today's public schools, Jonathan Kozol cites two New Jersey towns as examples. In mostly white Princeton, the board of education spent $7,725 per student during the 1988–1989 school year. The school board in nearby Camden, which is mostly African-American and Hispanic, spent an average of $3,538 to educate each pupil.

Elizabeth Eckford, one of the Little Rock Nine, stands by a statue of herself as a teenager that is part of a monument unveiled in 2005.

received. Today's lack of attention to the problem of relapsing into segregation makes the issue harder to resolve.

The U.S. Supreme Court's ruling on *Brown v. Board of Education* on May 17, 1954, was a giant leap forward for the civil rights movement. It was the initial step in

Brown Foundation

The Brown Foundation for Educational Equity, Excellence, and Research was established in 1988, led by the family of Oliver Brown. The Brown Foundation works to preserve the legacy of the Court's decision and to educate people about the history of the case. The Brown Foundation works in partnership with the Brown National Park.

breaking down racial barriers throughout the South, which has actually become the most integrated area in the United States. Moreover, the nine justices of the U.S. Supreme Court who unanimously ruled that school segregation was illegal gave a clear message with their decision: America needed to live out its creed that all men are created equal. After all, the creed applies to children as well. ⌐

Monroe School in Topeka, Kansas, was dedicated as the Brown v. Board of Education National Historic Site May 15, 2004, the fiftieth anniversary of the Supreme Court's ruling on the case.

TIMELINE

1865	1875	1896
The United States Supreme Court ratifies the Thirteenth Amendment to the Constitution December 6, freeing all slaves.	Congress passes the Civil Rights Act March 1 in an attempt to ban discrimination in public places.	The Supreme Court ruling in *Plessy v. Ferguson* May 18 establishes the "separate but equal" doctrine used to prevent integrated schools.

1949	1950	1951
The *Briggs v. Elliott* case, filed in South Carolina November 24, is the first of many that will eventually lead to the landmark *Brown v. Board of Education* decision.	The NAACP registers its first victory June 5 in the issue of school desegregation in a district court ruling in *Sweat v. Painter*.	The *Bolling v. Sharpe* suit is filed in Washington, D.C.

1899

The Supreme Court rules in *Cumming v. Richmond County* December 18 that courts cannot interfere with local school-board decisions.

1908

The Supreme Court forces Berea College to segregate its classes in *Berea College v. Kentucky* November 9.

1927

Mississippi is given the right by the Supreme Court November 21 to designate children as "white" or "colored" for the purpose of assigning them to public schools in its *Gong Lum v. Rice* ruling.

1951

The *Davis v. County School Board of Prince Edward County* suit is filed in Virginia May 31.

1951

The *Brown v. Board of Education* suit is filed in Kansas June 25.

1951

The *Belton v. Gebhart* and *Bulah v. Gebhart* lawsuits are filed in Delaware October 22.

TIMELINE

1952	1953	1954
Oral arguments are heard December 9 by the Supreme Court in *Brown v. Board of Education*.	Re-arguments in *Brown v. Board of Education* are heard December 7 by the Supreme Court.	The United States Senate confirms President Eisenhower's appointment of Earl Warren to the United States Supreme Court March 1.

1956	1957	1962
On February 24, Virginia politicians declare a policy of "massive resistance" to school desegregation that is adopted throughout the South.	Nine black students integrate Central High School in Little Rock, Arkansas, September 23, following months of resistance and protests.	James Meredith, an African American, registers as a student at the University of Mississippi October 1 following violent protests by white mobs.

1954

The Supreme Court issues its landmark decision in *Brown v. Board of Education (Brown I)* May 17, banning legal school segregation in America.

1955

A second ruling by the Supreme Court on the case of *Brown v. Board of Education (Brown II)* May 31 decrees that desegregation of schools can proceed with "all deliberate speed."

1955

In Montgomery, Alabama, Rosa Parks refuses to give up her seat on a bus December 1, sparking a boycott and the civil rights movement.

1964

The Supreme Court rules in *Griffin v. County School Board of Prince Edward County* May 25 that a school board may not close a school to avoid desegregation.

1964

President Lyndon Johnson signs the Civil Rights Act July 2, banning segregation in all public places.

1971

The Supreme Court votes unanimously April 20 that busing may be used as a tool to achieve school desegregation.

Essential Facts

DATE OF EVENT

May 17, 1954

PLACE OF EVENT

Washington, D.C

KEY PLAYERS

❖ Thurgood Marshall

❖ National Association for the Advancement of Colored People (NAACP)

❖ United States Supreme Court

❖ Countless individuals and families who lived with and fought segregation

HIGHLIGHTS OF EVENT

❖ Supreme Court ruling in *Plessy v. Ferguson* May 18, 1896, established the "separate but equal" doctrine used to segregate public schools.

❖ *Briggs v. Elliott* school desegregation lawsuit was filed November 24, 1949, in South Carolina.

❖ *Bolling v. Sharpe* school desegregation lawsuit was filed in 1951 in Washington, D.C.

❖ *Davis v. County School Board of Prince Edward County* was filed May 31, 1951, in Virginia to challenge the inadequacy of black schools.

❖ *Brown v. Board of Education* school desegregation suit was filed in Kansas June 21, 1951.

❖ *Belton v. Gebhart* and *Bulah v. Gebhart* school lawsuits were filed in Delaware on October 22, 1951, to challenge the inadequacy of black schools.

❖ Oral arguments in *Brown v. Board of Education* were heard December 9, 1952, by the Supreme Court.

❖ Re-arguments in *Brown v. Board of Education* were heard December 7, 1953, by the Supreme Court.

❖ The United States Senate confirmed President Eisenhower's appointment of Earl Warren to the United States Supreme Court March 1, 1954.

❖ Nine black students integrated Central High School in Little Rock, Arkansas, September 23, 1957, following months of resistance and protests.

❖ The Supreme Court issued its landmark decision May 17, 1954, in *Brown v. Board of Education (Brown I)*, banning legal school segregation in America.

❖ A second ruling by the Supreme Court on May 31, 1955, on *Brown v. Board of Education (Brown II)* decreed that desegregation of schools could proceed with "all deliberate speed."

❖ President Lyndon Johnson signed the Civil Rights Act July 2, 1964, banning segregation in all public places

QUOTE

"We come then to the question presented: Does segregation of children in public schools solely on the basis of race, even though the physical facilities and other 'tangible' factors may be equal, deprive the children of the minority group of equal educational opportunities? We believe that it does.

"We conclude that in the field of public education the doctrine of 'separate but equal' has no place. Separate educational facilities are inherently unequal. Therefore, we hold that the plaintiffs and others similarly situated for whom the actions have been brought are, by reason of the segregation complained of, deprived of the equal protection of the laws guaranteed by the Fourteenth Amendment."—Chief Justice Earl Warren, May 17, 1954

ABOUT THE AUTHOR

Marty Gitlin was a reporter for two newspapers in northeastern Ohio for 20 years before becoming solely a freelance writer. During his two decades as a reporter, Gitlin won more than 40 writing awards, including first place for general excellence from the Associated Press (AP) in 1995. AP also named him one of the top four feature writers in the state of Ohio in 2001.

PHOTO CREDITS

Bettmann/Corbis, cover, 3, 85, 87; AP Images, 15, 22, 33, 41, 42, 49, 50, 53, 57, 60, 65, 67, 68, 73, 77, 78, 96, 98, 99; Horace Cort/AP Images, 6, 97 (top); Brown Foundation for Educational Equity, Excellence, and Research, 16, 25, 97 (bottom); Lawrence Jackson/AP Images, 26, 59; Steve Helber/AP Images, 29; Courtesy of the NAACP/AP Images, 34; Danny Johnston/AP Images, 88, 93; Orlin Wagner/AP Images, 95